MOVING PICTURES

FIVE MID-INTERMEDIATE LEVEL PIANO SOLOS

BY NAOKO IKEDA

ISBN 978-1-4234-0731-7

EXCLUSIVELY DISTRIBUTED BY

7777 W. BLUEMOUND RD. P.O. BOX 13819 MILWAUKEE, WI 53213

In Australia Contact:
Hal Leonard Australia Pty. Ltd.
4 Lentara Court
Cheltenham, Victoria, 3192 Australia
Email: ausadmin@halleonard.com

Visit Hal Leonard Online at
www.halleonard.com

MOVING PICTURES
HOMAGE TO MONOCHROME CINEMA AND PIANO

I love watching old monochrome (black and white) movies and have a fondness for the atmosphere of times gone by. (These movies always come with wonderful music as well!) Black and white, light and shadow—I find these contrasts to be much more romantic than the ones in color. Our lovable piano is an instrument of black and white. We will soon use the eighty-eight keys found on our piano to create a special musical drama.

The collection's theme is monochrome. Each piece is stylistically different, but when played together as a set, resembles a mini soundtrack from a movie. I have placed important key words in each title to help guide you, but ultimately it is up to you, the performer, to assume the multiple roles of scriptwriter, director and main character, and to create your own moving pictures.

—Naoko Ikeda

CHROMATIC MONOCHROME
A MINOR 4/4 – MEDIUM FAST, STYLISHLY

At the beginning the main characters are introduced: the hero enters the scene first—followed a few measures later by the heroine at a higher octave. The two ranges clearly define the two different characters. Feel the rhythm of the bass and the beat while bringing out the melody. Ask yourself: Are these two on the same side or not? Is this a suspenseful thriller or an amusing comedy? Let the drama begin!

ROMANCE NOIR
D MAJOR 4/4 – ANDANTE, CON RUBATO ED ESPRESSIONE

Noir means black in French. In this piece I have tried to convey the deepness of, and fascination with, the color black. The key word is *romance*. As you play, try to find this *romance* by experimenting with several different takes on the sound of each phrase. It is often necessary for various takes by the director to get the perfect scene in a movie.

WHITE NOON
G MINOR 5/8+6/8 – ALLEGRETTO, FREELY

This piece involves a combination of 5/8 and 6/8 rhythms. When in 5/8 play as neatly and as evenly as you can, and when it switches to 6/8 play in a more sentimental style. The music moves freely and quickly, so stay in control of the rhythms. Be especially careful when playing 16th notes in the right hand to make sure that the left hand maintains a strong and steady rhythm.

FIREFLIES (HOTARU)
D MINOR 4/4 – ANDANTINO ARIOSO, IN A LYRIC STYLE

In Japan we have a unique custom that happens once a year, similar to the Thanksgiving holiday in the United States. Family members who live apart come home for a few days to spend time together and to perform customary rituals that are meant to comfort the spirits of their ancestors. This period is called *Bon*. It is held at the end of summer, and always at this time of year, the *hotaru* (fireflies) are in abundance. Imagine seeing hundreds of fireflies glimmering in the dark! This piece tries to describe that feeling of being in a fantasy land. As you play, note especially the dynamic contrasts, and play the arpeggios as effortlessly as possible. The image of the song is expressed in the following poem:

> In summer by clear water,
> I am the reason you keep coming back.
> I embrace you with radiant light, I convey how you feel.
> I am a firefly.
> And when the moment of farewell arrives,
> My soft glow will remind you of this beautiful summer.

> *(Poem translated by Takako Teranishi)*

CINEMATIC MONOCHROME
E-FLAT MAJOR 3/4 – MEDIUM SLOW, LINGERING AND SINGING

I would like to finish this drama cinematically. The frequent dynamic contrasts and tempo alterations reflect the many changes of expression in the final scene. Use your imagination to revisit your favorite scenes from the set and be sure to express your feelings.

For Akihito Teranishi

Chromatic Monochrome

Opening scene... Hero and Heroine enter.

Naoko Ikeda

Medium fast, stylishly

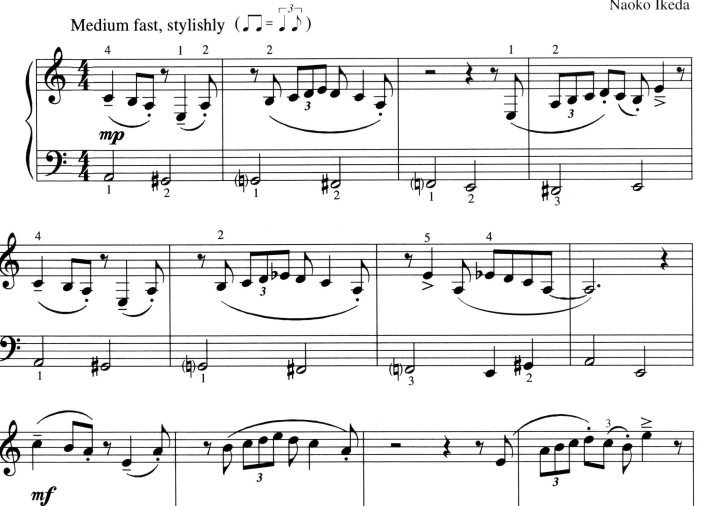

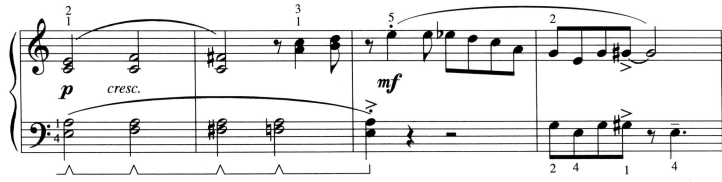

For Shima Sueoka

Romance Noir

Scene #1… Wonderful colors wait to be discovered beneath the black and white keys.

Naoko Ikeda

Andante, con rubato ed espressione

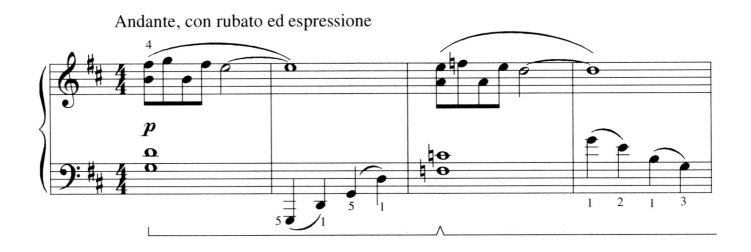

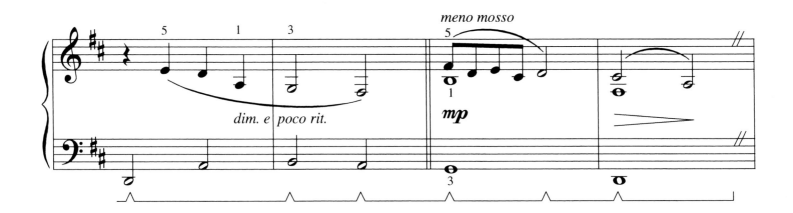

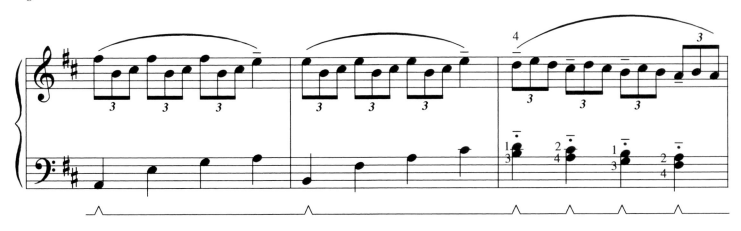

Tempo I

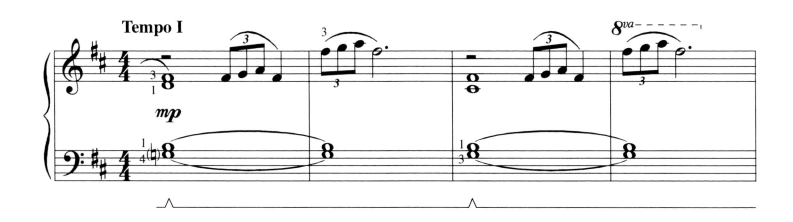

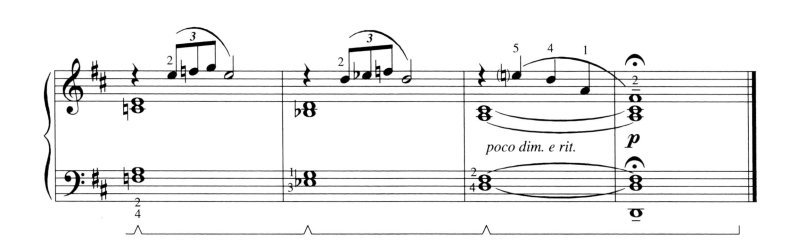

For Emiko Tanikawa

White Noon

Scene #2... An angel on the spiral staircase, bustle from the cities, a white labyrinth.

Naoko Ikeda

To Yukino Kitsuta

Fireflies (Hotaru)

Scene #3... Darkness and pale light...

Naoko Ikeda

Andantino arioso, in lyric style

Cinematic Monochrome

Closing scene… Again in a dream.

Naoko Ikeda

Medium slow, lingering and singing

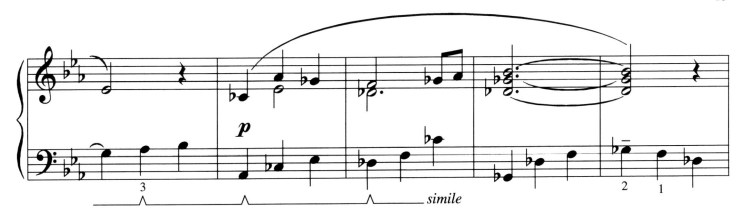

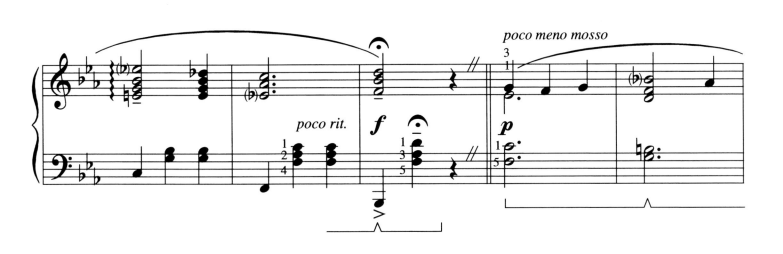

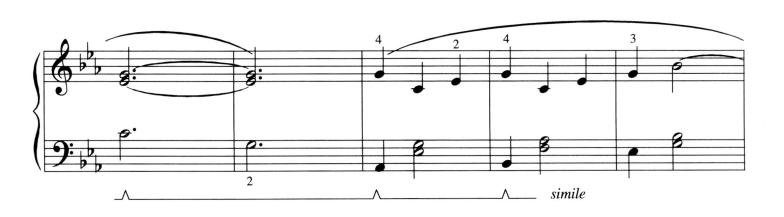

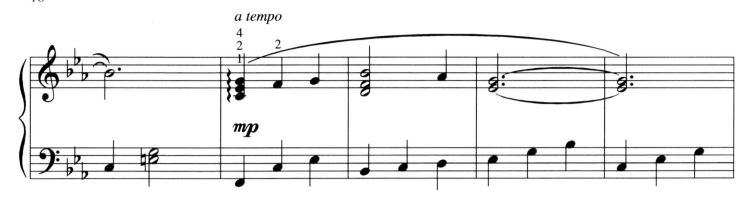

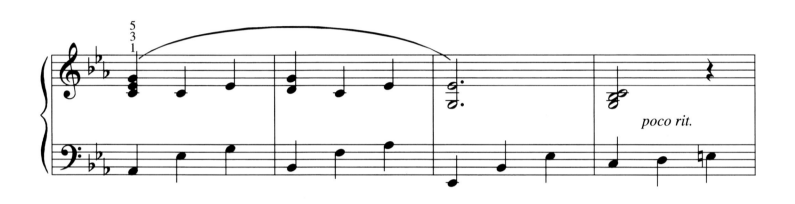

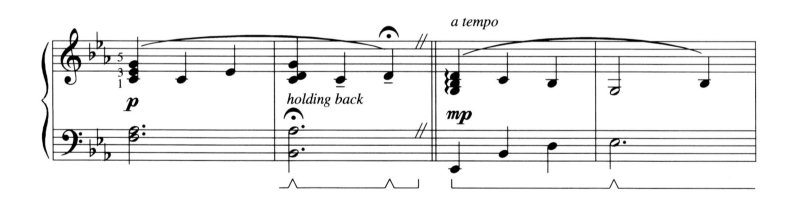

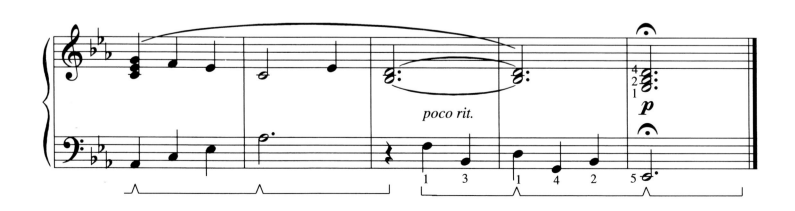